— THE GOURMET KITCHEN —
VINEGARS

WRITTEN BY GINA STEER
ILLUSTRATED BY ALISON BARRATT

THE
APPLE
PRESS

A QUARTO BOOK

Published by The Apple Press
6 Blundell Street
London N7 9BH

ISBN 1-85076-542-1

This book was designed and produced by
Quarto Publishing plc
The Old Brewery, 6 Blundell Street
London N7 9BH

Editors: Kate Kirby, Laura Washburn, Susan Ward
Art Editor: Mark Stevens
Designer: Julie Francis
Art Director: Moira Clinch
Editorial Director: Sophie Collins

Illustrations © Alison Barratt

Typeset in Great Britain by West End Studios, Eastbourne, UK
Manufactured in Hong Kong by Regent Publishing Services Ltd.
Printed in China by Leefung-Asco Printers Ltd.

Contents

INTRODUCTION

No kitchen is complete without a good selection of vinegars, whether they be basic vinegars, flavoured vinegars or a combination of the two. Vinegars offer a surprisingly wide range of uses: as a medium for pickling and preserving; as a flavour enhancer alone or in combination with other ingredients; as a tenderiser in marinades; and as an aromatic condiment, such as basil vinegar drizzled over tomato salad.

There was a time when the only vinegar sold in the supermarket was made from malt beer or cider. Thankfully, life has progressed considerably, as have the varieties of vinegar now available to the gourmet cook. Today, along with the usual

wine vinegars — white, red, champagne and sherry — and cider vinegars, there is a veritable host of flavours to choose from. The very names conjure up a wealth of gastronomic delights that positively tingle the taste buds — champagne, herb, berry, balsamic, garlic and peppercorn to name just a few.

As a rule, the choice of vinegar for any dish depends on the ethnic origins of the recipe. But one of the great beauties of cooking is its versatility. So try experimenting. Chefs do it, so why not you?

Other Uses of Vinegar

In addition to being an important ingredient in cooking, vinegar has other household uses. It can be used as an antiseptic for minor cuts and abrasions; for reducing the effect of insect bites and stings; or as an effective mouthwash and gargle, especially when combined with honey. (The latter is also particularly helpful for sore throats.) Try adding vinegar to bath water to help relieve aching tired muscles, or to rinse water to achieve beautiful shining hair.

What is Vinegar

Vinegar comes from the French *vin aigre,* meaning sour wine, but vinegar is also made from barley. Its development, a natural process, occurs when alcohol has been converted by acid-forming bacteria (much the same as milk is soured by lactic bacteria). The flavours found in the original wine or barley will impart either fruity or aromatic flavours to the vinegar.

Originally vinegar was made by leaving ale or wine standing in the open, where it 'turned' and became vinegar. Nowadays it is commercially brewed. First, starch in wine or barley is converted to sugar; then, added yeast turns the sugar to alcohol. Next, naturally occuring acetic acid bacterium (a vinegar 'mother') is added, encouraging bacteria to grow and turning the alcohol into vinegar. Finally, the vinegar is pumped into large vats where it is left to mature until ready for bottling.

Basic Vinegars

Wine vinegars are made from all types of wine from many different regions of the world. Though it may sound obvious, the better the wine, the better the vinegar. Even a particular type of wine vinegar can be made in a variety of ways. For example, sherry vinegar is made from sherry; it can be produced within a year or over a period of years, and it might be decanted into progressively smaller barrels in order to mature and deepen the flavor, as with a fine Cognac.

Balsamic vinegar, considered by many to be the ultimate vinegar, has been made in Modena, Italy since the 16th century. In those early days it was a valuable commodity and was often included in a bride's dowry or as a prized legacy in a will. Dark, rich, sweet and pungent, the superb flavour of balsamic vinegar is the result of the length and refinement of its ageing process. As with old Cognac, the wooden vats that store the vinegar are of paramount importance. The woods used in the construction of the vats may be oak, walnut or cherry, each imparting its distinctive taste. Traditionally, it takes ten years for the vinegar to mature.

The type of vinegar popular in a particular country — or even a particular region — depends upon local raw materials and drinking habits. Hence wine vinegar comes from the wine-producing areas, while English malt vinegar uses the malted barley commonly used to make beer. Cider vinegar, with its more acidic flavour, is produced from cider or fermented apple juice, and is typical of fruit-growing areas.

Chinese and Japanese rice vinegars vary in colour, from pale golden to almost clear. Milder than Western vinegars, Japanese vinegar is slightly sweeter. Chinese black vinegar can be made from wheat, millet or sorghum and, like the European balsamic version, the best is matured for several years. It should have a pleasantly bitter taste and a distinctive smoky flavour.

Flavoured Vinegars

The selection of flavoured vinegars that graces supermarket and delicatessen shelves today outstrips the imagination. Garlic, mixed herb and peppercorn, blackcurrant and raspberry are only four from a long catalogue.

What could be better than a tomato and mozzarella salad drizzled with dressing made from basil-flavoured vinegar or a home-made lentil soup perked up with a dash of dill vinegar? Rosemary vinegar can serve as a fragrant dressing for chicken salad or can be used to deglaze the pan after roasting a chicken. In commercially made flavoured vinegars, the flavouring herbs, spices or fruits are steeped in the vinegar for an extended time — longer than two years.

For home-made flavoured vinegars, a walk through your garden or a trip to the greengrocer can yield a harvest of new flavours. Pick a bunch of lavender flowers or scented roses; shake to dislodge any insects; rinse and air dry; then trim the stalks. Pack the flowers or petals into sterilised jars, cover with white wine vinegar, seal and leave in the dark for at least 1 month. Strain before use.

You can also use violet petals to give subtle flavour, while nasturtium seeds impart a strong caper-like taste. Try steeping vanilla pods, shavings of coconut or horseradish, strips of citrus fruit zest, and even peanuts. The choice is yours.

Making Your Own Vinegar

To make your own vinegar, you must first make a vinegar 'mother'. Place 2 tablespoons of vinegar and half a bottle of wine or cider in a bowl and then leave in a sunny place — a window sill will do nicely — for two weeks. The skin that forms (the aceto bacteria) is the vinegar 'mother', which is the starter that is needed to turn wine (or other alcohols) into vinegar.

Skim off the 'mother' and transfer it — with more of the same type of alcohol — to a wide-mouthed container; or bowl. Cover the opening with muslin ensuring that it receives a good supply of oxygen, and leave the filled container in a warm place. After 1 month, strain out the vinegar. The 'mother' can be kept and the process repeated indefinitely as long as fresh alcohol is added to feed the 'mother'. To make flavoured vinegars, immediately after straining steep the flavouring of your choice in the strained vinegar. Leave for as long as possible before use. Once opened, store in a cool place.

STARTERS

Fresh Figs with Edible Flowers

4 ripe figs

115g/4oz cottage cheese

8 thin slices smoked chicken

Few radicchio and chicory leaves

Few round lettuce leaves

Few edible flowers

Dressing

4 tablespoons sunflower oil

3 tablespoons cider and honey
  vinegar

½ teaspoon mustard powder

¼ teaspoon each salt and freshly
  ground black pepper

3 tablespoons fromage frais

*W*ipe the figs, then quarter them without cutting through. Open up and place a mound of cheese in the centre of each fig.

Form the smoked chicken slices into rolls. Divide the endive and lettuce leaves among the plates and arrange the chicken rolls on top. Garnish with edible flowers.

Mix the dressing ingredients and serve with the salads. *Serves 4.*

Scallops Ceviche

8 large scallops (fresh or fully
   thawed), cleaned
180ml/6floz lime juice
3 tablespoons sherry vinegar,
   or lemon grass vinegar
115–170g/4–6oz salad leaves
1 teaspoon grated lime zest

Salsa
3 tablespoons sunflower oil

1 tablespoon tomato paste
1 tablespoon sherry vinegar
1 fresh green chilli, seeded, and
   finely chopped
3 ripe tomatoes, peeled, seeded
   and chopped
3 spring onions, trimmed and finely
   chopped
Dash Tabasco sauce
1/4 teaspoon salt

Lightly rinse the scallops and place in a glass bowl. Blend the lime juice and vinegar, pour over the scallops, cover and marinate in the refrigerator for at least 12 hours. Stir occasionally.

For the salsa, blend the oil, tomato paste and vinegar together. Stir in the chopped chilli, tomatoes, spring onions, Tabasco sauce, and salt. Mix lightly, then set aside for 1 hour.

Drain the scallops, arrange them on a bed of salad leaves and garnish with the lime zest. Serve with the salsa. *Serves 4.*

NOTE When planning to eat shellfish raw, purchase only from a reputable fishmonger. Be sure shellfish is commercially farmed, fresh and clean.

Clams Marinière

900g/2lb clams or mussels
1 tablespoon salt
150ml/¼ pint dry white wine
1 onion, sliced
1 small lemon, sliced
30g/1oz parsley chopped
2 bay leaves
10 peppercorns, lightly bruised
150ml/¼ pint water
3 tablespoons sherry vinegar or red wine vinegar
4 tablespoons single cream

Discard any clams or mussels that are open or damaged. Scrub thoroughly in plenty of cold water. Place clams in a large bowl, cover with salted water and allow to stand for 30 minutes. (Do not soak mussels.) While clams are soaking, place the wine, onion, lemon, half the parsley, the bay leaves, peppercorns and water in a large saucepan. Bring to the boil over high heat, then reduce heat and simmer gently for 15 minutes.

Rinse and drain the clams.

14

Add clams or mussels to the pan. Cover and cook on high heat for 7–10 minutes or until all the shells have opened. Holding the lid tightly, shake the pan frequently, or stir the clams or mussels with a wooden spoon.

Using a slotted spoon, remove the clams or mussels to a serving bowl, discarding any that have not opened; keep warm. Strain the liquid remaining in the pan and return it to the cleaned pan. Bring to the boil and cook vigorously on high heat for 5 minutes or until reduced by half. Reduce heat, add the vinegar and cook for a further 2 minutes. Remove the pan from the heat, stir in the cream and remaining parsley, pour over the clams and serve immediately.

Serves 4.

Insalata di Funghi

3 tablespoons garlic-flavoured olive oil
1–2 cloves garlic, crushed
1–2 fresh green chillies, seeded and chopped
115g/4oz each chanterelle, oyster and button mushrooms,
wiped and thickly sliced
4 tablespoons white or red wine vinegar
Pinch of salt and ½ teaspoon freshly ground black pepper
1 tablespoon chopped fresh flat-leaved parsley
Few shavings black truffle, optional
1 tablespoon fresh chives, finely chopped
1 teaspoon orange zest, cut into julienne strips

*H*eat the oil and gently sauté the garlic and chillies over moderate heat for 3 minutes. Add the mushrooms and continue to cook for 3 minutes or until the mushrooms have softened slightly. Stir in the vinegar, seasoning and parsley. Serve warm, sprinkled with a few shavings of black truffle, if liked. Garnish with the chives and orange zest. *Serves 4.*

Fresh Pear, Brie & Pecan Medley

4 ripe pears
3 tablespoons lemon juice
About 170g/6oz ripe Brie
Few frisée and rocket leaves
60g/2oz pecan nut halves
115g/4oz wild strawberries

Dressing
4 tablespoons crème fraîche
1 teaspoon whole grain mustard
5 tablespoons extra-virgin olive oil
4 tablespoons champagne vinegar or
    red wine vinegar
1 teaspoon green peppercorns

*W*ipe the pears and cut them in half. Discard the core. Slice the pears thinly and brush with lemon juice. Cut the Brie into thin slivers. Arrange the salad leaves and pears on four individual serving plates, with the Brie slices on top. Sprinkle with the pecans and strawberries.

Mix together the crème fraîche and mustard. Gradually stir in the oil, vinegar and peppercorns. Drizzle over the pears and serve immediately. *Serves 4.*

Chinese Hot & Sour Soup

115g/4oz carrots, peeled

2 stalks celery, trimmed

10cm/4in piece cucumber, peeled and seeded

115g/4oz shiitake mushrooms

1 tablespoon olive oil

1 litre/1¾ pints chicken stock

3 tablespoons rice vinegar

1 tablespoon soy sauce

1 tablespoon dry sherry

1 clove garlic, crushed

1–2 fresh green chillies, seeded if preferred and finely sliced

2 teaspoons peeled and grated fresh root ginger

115g/4oz mange-touts, trimmed

115g/4oz canned bamboo shoots, sliced

1 rounded tablespoon cornflour

4 tablespoons water

3 tablespoons Chinese black vinegar or balsamic vinegar

3 spring onions, trimmed and sliced diagonally

Cut the carrot, celery and cucumber into julienne strips. Wipe or lightly rinse the mushrooms and cut into 5mm/ ¼in slices. Heat the oil in a frying pan over moderately high heat and lightly sauté the mushrooms for 2 minutes or until just softened. Drain on paper towels, squeezing out any excess oil, and reserve.

Place the stock, rice vinegar, soy sauce and sherry in a large pan with the garlic, chillies and ginger. Bring to the boil over high heat, then reduce to a simmer. Add the carrot and celery and cook for 2 minutes, then add the cucumber, mushrooms, mange-touts and bamboo shoots.

Mix the cornflour to a smooth paste with the water. Bring the soup to the boil over high heat, then stir in the cornflour paste. Continue to stir over high heat until the soup thickens, then add the vinegar. Serve piping hot, sprinkled with the spring onion garnish. *Serves 4.*

Mussels with Lemon Grass

16 mussels, cooked in their shells

2–3 lemon grass stalks, chopped

2 fresh green chillies, seeded
and sliced

2 cloves garlic, crushed or
finely chopped

1 tablespoon capers, coarsely chopped

3 tablespoons white wine vinegar
or lemon grass vinegar

4 tablespoons sunflower oil

1/2 teaspoon honey

Few fresh coriander leaves, chopped

Shell the mussels and place in a shallow dish. Wash, dry and reserve the shells. Place the lemon grass, 1 chilli, garlic, capers, vinegar, oil and honey in a saucepan. Bring to the boil and cook on high heat for 3 minutes. Stir in most of the coriander. When cool, pour over the mussels, cover and chill for at least 1 hour.

To serve, drain the mussels and replace in their shells. Strain the marinade and drizzle a little over each mussel. Garnish with the remaining coriander and chilli, and serve. *Serves 4.*

20

Melon with Parma Ham & Passion Fruit Dressing

1 Galia melon, peeled and seeded
8 thin slices Parma ham
Few radicchio and sorrel leaves
225g/8oz feta cheese, cubed
Few nasturtium blossoms

Dressing
3 ripe passion fruits
Pinch each of mustard powder, salt and freshly ground black pepper
2 tablespoons champagne vinegar or oregano-flavoured white wine vinegar
4 tablespoons fromage frais

Cut the melon into 8 wedges. Roll a strip of ham around each melon wedge. Decorate a serving platter with the salad leaves and arrange the wedges on top. Sprinkle the cheese on top.

Rub the passion fruit pulp through a sieve set on a bowl. Stir in the mustard, seasoning and vinegar. Blend in the soft cheese. Drizzle a little of the dressing over the melon salad and serve the rest separately. Garnish with the flower blossoms. *Serves 4.*

MAIN-COURSE SALADS

Warm Potato Salad

340g/12oz baby red potatoes
225g/8oz baby carrots
2 very small Spanish or red onions,
    thinly sliced
170g/6oz seedless grapes, halved
1 green dessert apple
115–170g/4–6oz mixed salad leaves
2 teaspoons finely chopped fresh
    chives

Dressing

4 tablespoons herb vinegar
4 tablespoons walnut oil
1 teaspoon whole grain mustard
2 teaspoons orange blossom
    honey
¼ teaspoon salt and ½ teaspoon
    freshly ground black pepper

Scrub the potatoes and carrots. Cook separately in lightly salted boiling water over high heat until tender. Drain. Cut the potatoes into halves or quarters, if large; cut the carrots in half. Place potatoes and carrots in a bowl with the onion and grapes. Core and chop the apple and add to the vegetables. Line a salad bowl with the salad leaves and fill with the potato mixture.

In a saucepan over moderate heat, stir together the vinegar, oil, mustard, honey and the seasoning. Pour the warm dressing over the potato salad. Garnish with the chives. *Serves 4.*

Smoked Salmon with Raspberries

225g/8oz fresh asparagus, trimmed
   and sliced diagonally
1 tablespoon walnut oil
2 ripe avocados
2 tablespoons lemon juice
Mixture of radicchio, frisée
   and rocket leaves
225g/8oz smoked salmon or trout,
   cut into strips

115g/4oz fresh raspberries
Few pecorino cheese shavings

Dressing

4 tablespoons raspberry vinegar
3 tablespoons walnut oil
½ teaspoon mustard powder
120ml/4floz soured cream

Sauté the asparagus in the oil over moderate heat for 5 minutes, stirring frequently; drain and set aside. Peel and dice the avocados, sprinkle with lemon juice and reserve. Arrange the salad leaves on a platter. Top with the asparagus, avocado, fish and raspberries.

Blend the vinegar, oil and mustard until well mixed; stir in the soured cream. Drizzle the dressing over the salad. Top with cheese shavings and serve. *Serves 4.*

Warm Asparagus & Chanterelle Salad

7 tablespoons virgin olive oil

340g/12oz fresh asparagus, trimmed and sliced diagonally

225g/8oz fresh chanterelles, wiped and sliced

1 clove garlic, crushed

225g/8oz baby spinach, rinsed

3 tablespoons pine nuts, toasted

60g/2oz oil-packed sun-dried tomatoes, chopped

3 tablespoons balsamic or red wine vinegar

½ teaspoon mustard powder

½ teaspoon caster sugar

¼ teaspoon sea salt and ½ teaspoon

freshly ground black pepper

Few shavings black truffle (optional)

1 orange, cut into small wedges

*H*eat 1 tablespoon of the oil in a frying pan over moderate heat. Sauté the asparagus for 5 minutes; drain and reserve. In the same pan, sauté the mushrooms and garlic in 4 tablespoons oil for 2 minutes or until softened. Add the spinach and cook for 30 seconds or just

24

until wilted. Return the asparagus to the pan, adding the pine nuts and sun-dried tomatoes. Transfer to a serving dish.

Mix the remaining 2 tablespoons oil with the vinegar, mustard, sugar and seasoning in a bowl. Pour over the salad and toss lightly. Sprinkle with shavings of truffle, if using, and garnish with the orange wedges. *Serves 4.*

Salmon Kebabs with Cucumber Salsa

450g/1lb fresh salmon fillet, skinned and cut into 4cm/1½in cubes

2 shallots, finely sliced

2 bay leaves

Few parsley sprigs

5 white peppercorns, lightly crushed

5 tablespoons tarragon vinegar

3 tablespoons virgin olive oil

2 limes, cut into 8 wedges

Few tarragon sprigs

2 teaspoons grated lime zest

Salsa

½ small cucumber, peeled, seeded and finely chopped

1 clove garlic, crushed

4 spring onions, trimmed and chopped

2 ripe tomatoes, peeled, seeded, drained and chopped

1 tablespoon tarragon vinegar

1 tablespoon lime juice

¼ teaspoon each salt and freshly ground black pepper

Arrange the salmon in a shallow dish. Sprinkle with the sliced shallots, herbs and peppercorns. Mix the vinegar and oil together, pour the mixture over the salmon, cover and

26

marinate in the refrigerator for at least 30 minutes to allow the flavors to develop.

Meanwhile, make the salsa. Place the cucumber in a bowl with the garlic, spring onions and tomatoes; add the vinegar, lime juice and seasoning. Mix well, then cover and set aside so that the flavours can develop.

Drain the salmon and thread alternately with the lime wedges on to skewers. Brush with the remaining marinade and cook under a preheated grill for 3–4 minutes, turning at least once. Brush again with the marinade to keep the salmon moist and succulent. Garnish with the tarragon and lime zest and serve with the cucumber salsa. *Serves 4.*

Lobster with Champagne Sauce

1 onion, sliced

1 large carrot, peeled and sliced

2 stalks celery, trimmed and chopped

1 bouquet garni

Few parsley sprigs

150ml/¼ pint champagne or dry white wine

3 tablespoons champagne vinegar

2 live lobsters

Few mixed salad leaves

2 pink grapefruits, peeled and segmented

10cm/4in piece cucumber, peeled, seeded and cut into 5cm/2in julienne strips

Caviar

Sauce

2 shallots, peeled and chopped

300ml/½ pint champagne

15g/½oz unsalted butter

2 tablespoons plain flour

1 tablespoon champagne vinegar

120ml/4floz soured cream

Pinch of salt

½ teaspoon freshly ground white pepper

*P*lace the onion, carrot, celery, herbs, champagne or white wine, and vinegar in a large pan. Add 300ml/½ pint water, bring to the boil and simmer gently for 10 minutes. Return to the boil, add the lobsters, cover and cook for about 15 minutes over moderate heat or until the lobsters have turned red-orange. Remove from heat and allow to cool for 5 minutes. Transfer the lobsters to a platter and let sit until cool enough to handle. Cut the lobsters in half lengthways, remove the meat, discarding the inedible parts, and cut into bite-size pieces.

Rinse the shells and line with salad leaves. Mix the lobster meat with the grapefruit and cucumber and return to the shells.

Place the shallots in a pan with the champagne and boil until the liquid reduces to about 180ml/6floz. Strain and discard the shallots. Mix the butter and flour together to form a paste. Bring the reduced champagne to the boil, then whisk in small pieces of the butter paste. Cook, whisking constantly, until thickened. Remove from the heat and stir in the vinegar, soured cream and seasoning. Return to a low heat to warm.

Drizzle a little sauce over the lobsters and garnish with caviar just before serving. Serve warm or cold with the remaining sauce. *Serves 4.*

MAIN DISHES

Piquant Chicken with Pink Grapefruit

4 chicken breasts, skinned and boned

3 tablespoons virgin olive oil

4 tablespoons red wine vinegar or grapefruit vinegar

1 tablespoon soy sauce

2 tablespoons redcurrant jelly

2 cloves garlic, crushed

2 pink grapefruits, peeled and segmented

Pinch of sea salt and ½ teaspoon freshly ground black pepper

1 teaspoon cornflour

3 tablespoons water

115-170g/4–6oz salad leaves

Few chervil sprigs

Rinse and dry the chicken breasts and place them in a shallow dish. In a saucepan over moderate heat, combine the olive oil, vinegar, soy sauce, jelly and garlic, stirring until smooth. Cool slightly, then pour the mixture over the chicken. Cover and marinate in the refrigerator for at least 1 hour.

Heat the oven to 200°C/400°F/gas mark 6 about 15 minutes before cooking. Drain the chicken, reserving the marinade, and place each breast on a small square of foil. Pour a little marinade over the chicken, then fold the foil into packets. Bake the packets for 15–20 minutes or until cooked. Five minutes before the end of cooking time, turn back the foil and distribute the grapefruit segments over the chicken breasts.

Place the reserved marinade in a small saucepan with the seasoning and bring to the boil. Blend the cornflour to a smooth paste with the water; add it to the marinade and cook over high heat, stirring, until smooth and thickened. Arrange the salad leaves on a platter. Transfer the chicken and grapefruit to the platter and pour the sauce over. Garnish with the chervil. *Serves 4.*

NOTE This dish also works well with duck breasts.

Turkey, Mushroom & Cranberry Stir-fry

5 tablespoons sunflower oil

450g/1lb boneless turkey breast, cubed

1 Spanish or red onion, peeled and cut into 2.5cm/1in pieces

2 cloves garlic, crushed

115g/4oz fresh chanterelle, oyster and button mushrooms,
wiped and thickly sliced

120ml/4floz turkey or chicken stock

5 tablespoons orange juice

45g/1½oz soft brown sugar

125g/4½oz fresh cranberries

2 teaspoons cornflour

3 tablespoons balsamic vinegar

½ tablespoon chopped fresh coriander

*H*eat 3 tablespoons of the oil in a wok. Sauté the turkey in batches for 5 minutes, stirring frequently. Drain and reserve. Add 1 tablespoon of the oil to the pan and sauté the onion and garlic for 2–3 minutes; drain and reserve. Stir in the remaining oil and the mushrooms and continue cooking for 1 minute. Return the turkey and onions to the wok

along with the stock, orange juice, sugar and cranberries. Bring to the boil, then cover and simmer for 5 minutes or until the cranberries just begin to 'pop'. Meanwhile, blend the cornflour with the vinegar to form a paste. Add to the wok and cook for 1 minute or until thickened. Serve garnished with the coriander. *Serves 4.*

NOTE This recipe will work well if either chicken or beef fillet is substitued for the turkey. Or vary the type of mushrooms used — try shiitake or any other variety.

Duck Breasts with Kumquats

4 duck breast halves, boned

1 tablespoon sunflower oil

2 cloves garlic, crushed

1–2 fresh green chillies, seeded and
  chopped

1 onion, thinly sliced

2 teaspoons whole grain mustard

¼ teaspoon salt and ½ teaspoon
  freshly ground black pepper

1 tablespoon soft brown sugar

4 tablespoons cider and honey vinegar

150ml/¼ pint chicken or vegetable
  stock

About 150g/5oz kumquats, halved

4 spring onions, trimmed and sliced
  diagonally

Few coriander sprigs

Rinse and dry the duck breasts and make 3 deep slashes across the skin. Heat the oil in a large frying pan and brown the duck on all sides over moderately high heat. Remove from the pan and drain on paper towels. Pour off all but 1 tablespoon fat, add the garlic, chillies, and onion to the pan, and sauté over moderate heat for 3 minutes or until slightly softened. Stir in the whole grain mustard, seasoning, sugar, vinegar and stock. Bring to the boil, then reduce the heat. Return the duck

34

to the pan, cover and simmer over low heat for 15 minutes. Add all but 2 kumquats to the pan and continue simmering for 5 minutes or until the duck is tender.

Blanch the spring onions in boiling water for 2 minutes, then drain. Slice the reserved kumquats. Arrange the duck on a warmed serving platter, pour the sauce over and garnish with the spring onions, coriander and remaining 2 kumquats sliced. Serve with freshly cooked pasta and a mixed green salad. *Serves 4.*

NOTE Try substituting stoned fresh cherries, when they are in season, for the kumquats.

Italian Calf's Liver

450g/1lb calf's liver, deveined

1 onion, sliced

2 bay leaves, coarsely torn

Few parsley sprigs

Few fresh sage leaves

5 peppercorns, lightly crushed

1 tablespoon redcurrant jelly, warmed

4 tablespoons walnut oil

4 tablespoons sherry vinegar or sage vinegar

3 tablespoons seasoned flour

2 cloves garlic, crushed

1 each red and orange peppers, seeded and sliced

3 tablespoons coarsely chopped sun-dried tomatoes

2 teaspoons soy sauce

150ml/¼ pint chicken stock

½ teaspoon freshly ground black pepper

½ tablespoon coarsely chopped fresh sage leaves

Cut the liver into very thin slices and place in a shallow dish. Scatter the onion, bay leaves, parsley, sage and peppercorns on top. Mix the jelly, 1 tablespoon of the oil and the vinegar together. Pour the mixture over the liver, cover and marinate in the refrigerator for 30 minutes, turning at least once.

Remove the liver from the marinade; strain the liquid, and reserve. Coat the liver in the seasoned flour. Add the remaining oil to a frying pan over moderate heat. Sauté the garlic and bell peppers for 5 minutes; remove with a slotted spoon and reserve. Add the liver, turn the heat to high and brown on all sides. Return the garlic and peppers to the pan and add the reserved marinade, the sun-dried tomatoes, soy sauce and stock. Bring to the boil, then reduce heat and simmer for 5 minutes or until the liver is cooked. Add the pepper and serve garnished with the sage. *Serves 4.*

Lamb with Apricot Relish

4 lamb cutlets
1 teaspoon crushed garlic
1 tablespoon hazelnut oil
3 tablespoons cider vinegar
3 tablespoons apricot nectar or orange juice
3 bay leaves, coarsely torn
Few mint sprigs
1 tablespoon green peppercorns
4 fresh apricots

Relish

115g/4oz dried apricots, finely chopped
150ml/¼ pint apricot nectar or orange juice
3 tablespoons cider vinegar
1 tablespoon soft dark brown sugar
1 teaspoon ground cinnamon
½ teaspoon freshly grated nutmeg
Small knob butter

Place the lamb cutlets in a shallow dish. Mix the garlic, oil, vinegar, fruit juice, bay leaves, some of the mint sprigs and the peppercorns and pour the mixture over the lamb. Cover and marinate in the refrigerator for at least 1 hour.

Preheat the grill to high. Drain the lamb cutlets and place on the grill rack. Brush with a little marinade, then grill on each side for 2 minutes. Reduce the heat to moderate and continue to grill for 6–8 minutes on each side or until cooked.

Meanwhile, make the relish. Place the dried apricots in a pan with the fruit juice, vinegar and sugar. Simmer gently over low heat for 10–15 minutes, then purée until smooth and thick. Add the cinnamon, nutmeg and butter and stir well. Serve spooned over the lamb chops, garnished with halved fresh apricots and more mint sprigs.
Serves 4.

Pork Medallions with Plum Sauce

450g/1lb boned pork loin, cut into 8 medallions
each about 2.5cm/1in thick
2 cloves garlic, crushed
4½ tablespoons dry white wine
3 tablespoons sweet blackberry vinegar (see page 61)
1 tablespoon safflower oil
Few flat-leaved parsley sprigs

Sauce

340g/12oz dark red plums, stoned
3 tablespoons redcurrant jelly
7 tablespoons water
1 tablespoon hoisin sauce
½–1 teaspoon arrowroot
2 tablespoons balsamic vinegar

Place the pork in a shallow dish and sprinkle on garlic. Mix the wine, vinegar and oil; pour over the pork, cover and marinate in the refrigerator for at least 30 minutes. Just before cooking, preheat the grill to high. Drain the pork, place on the grill rack and cook for 2 minutes on each side. Reduce the heat to moderate and continue

40

cooking for 3–4 minutes on each side or until cooked to your liking.

Wash the plums. Reserve 2 for garnish and coarsely chop the remainder. Place them in a saucepan with the jelly and 4 tablespoons of water. Bring to the boil, then reduce the heat to low and simmer for 10 minutes or until the plums are soft. Sieve, discard plum skins and return to the pan. Add the hoisin sauce and bring back to the boil. Blend the arrowroot with 3 tablespoons water, stir into the sauce and cook over high heat until it is clear and thickened. Turn down the heat, add the balsamic vinegar, stir until well blended and transfer to a sauceboat.

Garnish the pork with slices of reserved plum and parsley sprigs, and accompany with the sauce. *Serves 4.*

Seafood Brochettes

450g/1lb fresh seafood of one
    variety, such as monkfish, salmon,
    tuna or raw king prawns
Few dill sprigs
2 cloves garlic, crushed
6 tablespoons champagne vinegar
4 tablespoons virgin olive oil

Grated zest and juice of 1/2 lemon
Pinch of salt and 1/2 teaspoon freshly
    ground black pepper
4 tablespoons sesame seeds
Few bay leaves
4 each lemon and lime wedges

*D*iscard the bones and skin from the fish and cut into cubes. If using prawns, remove the shell — except for the tail — and remove the fine legs and dark intestinal membrane. Place the seafood in a shallow dish and sprinkle with some dill and the garlic. Mix the vinegar, oil, lemon zest and juice and seasoning. Pour over the fish, cover and chill for at least 30 minutes.

Preheat grill to high. Drain the seafood, reserving marinade, roll in sesame seeds and thread on to skewers, interspersed with bay leaves. Brush the brochettes with marinade and grill, turning frequently and brushing with more marinade, for 5 minutes or until just cooked. Garnish with more dill and lemon and lime wedges. *Serves 4.*

Chicken Breasts with Pink Peppercorns

4 chicken breasts, skinned and boned

1 tablespoon sunflower oil

3 tablespoons raspberry vinegar

1 tablespoon acacia honey

Grated zest and juice of 1 large orange

Few mint sprigs

3 tablespoons pink peppercorns

Few fresh raspberries

*R*inse and dry the chicken breasts. Heat the oil in a frying pan over high heat and seal the meat. Remove from the heat, lift out the breasts and wipe the pan clean. Return the chicken to the pan. Mix the vinegar, honey and grated orange zest and juice and drizzle the mixture over the chicken. Add some of the mint, bruised, and the peppercorns to the pan, and bring to the boil. Reduce the heat to low, cover and simmer gently for 15–20 minutes, turning once or twice, until the chicken is cooked. Discard the mint. Arrange the chicken on a warmed platter and pour the pan juices on top. Garnish with more mint and some raspberries. *Serves 4.*

Beef Fillet in Piquant Vinegar Sauce

4 thick slices of beef fillet (about 340g/12oz), trimmed

2 cloves garlic, crushed

1 tablespoon chopped mixed herbs, such as thyme,
oregano, sage and parsley

¼ teaspoon salt and ½ teaspoon freshly ground black pepper

5 tablespoons red wine vinegar

2 teaspoons honey

150ml/¼ pint red wine

1 tablespoon tomato paste

1 teaspoon arrowroot

1 tablespoon water

1 teaspoon soft brown sugar

½ tablespoon chopped flat-leaved parsley

1 leaf frisée, shredded

Place the slices of beef in a shallow dish. In a bowl, mix the garlic, herbs, seasoning, vinegar, honey, red wine and tomato paste. Stir well to blend, pour on top of the beef and cover. Marinate for 1 hour in the refrigerator.

Preheat the grill to high. Place the meat on the grill

44

rack and grill for about 2 minutes on each side to brown. Turn down the grill to moderate and continue to cook for 3 minutes on each side or until done to your liking.

Strain the marinade, bring to the boil and cook on high for 5 minutes or until reduced by half. Blend the arrowroot with the water, stir into the marinade with the sugar and cook until thickened. Pour it over the beef and sprinkle with the parsley and frisée. *Serves 4.*

Turkey Brochettes with Apple & Orange Salsa

340g/12oz boneless, skinless turkey breast

Pinch of salt and ½ teaspoon freshly ground black pepper

4 tablespoons sunflower oil

4 tablespoons cider and honey vinegar

2 teaspoons soy sauce

2 teaspoons wildflower or orange blossom honey, warmed

120ml/4floz apple or orange juice

1 medium onion, sliced

2 cloves garlic, crushed

1 medium red apple, cored and cut into wedges

1 medium orange, cut into wedges

Few mint sprigs

Salsa

1 small green apple, cored

1 large orange, peeled and segmented

1 small Spanish or red onion, peeled

1 tablespoon cider and honey vinegar

1 tablespoon finely chopped fresh mint

Pinch of salt and ¼ teaspoon freshly ground black pepper

Rinse the turkey and pat dry with paper towels. Cut into 4cm/1½in cubes and place in a shallow dish. Season with the salt and pepper. Mix together the oil, vinegar, soy sauce, honey and juice, then pour the mixture over the turkey. Sprinkle with the onion and garlic, cover and marinate in the refrigerator for at least 1 hour, stirring occasionally.

To make the salsa, finely chop the green apple, orange and onion. Mix well, then drain and place in a bowl. Mix in the remaining ingredients. Cover and chill for 30 minutes to allow the flavours to develop.

Drain the turkey, then thread on to skewers alternately with the red apple and orange wedges. Brush with the marinade. Grill for 8–10 minutes or until cooked, turning at least once and brushing occasionally with the marinade. Garnish with mint sprigs and serve with the salsa. *Serves 4.*

Pot-roasted Chicken with Grapes

1 free-range chicken (about 1.4kg/3lb)

Few thyme, sage, oregano and rosemary sprigs,
tied in a bunch

1 medium onion, quartered

2 carrots, peeled and thickly sliced

1 fennel bulb, trimmed and cut into thick wedges

½ teaspoon each salt and freshly ground black pepper

4 tablespoons white wine vinegar or oregano-flavoured white wine vinegar

300ml/½ pint chicken stock or white wine

30g/1oz butter or margarine, softened

4 tablespoons plain flour

115g/4oz seedless grapes, skinned if preferred and halved

4 tablespoons single cream

Few oregano or chervil sprigs

Preheat the oven to 190°C/375°F/gas mark 5. Rinse and dry the chicken and place the bunch of herbs inside it. Arrange the prepared vegetables in the bottom of a chicken brick or casserole. Season the chicken with half the salt and pepper and place it in the brick or casserole. Mix the vinegar with the stock and pour it over. Cover the casserole and bake for 1½ hours or until thoroughly cooked. Transfer the chicken and vegetables to a platter and keep warm.

Strain the pan juices into a saucepan and add enough water to make up to 600ml/1 pint. Bring to the boil over high heat. Beat the butter and flour together to make a paste. Drop small pieces of it into the pan juices, whisking vigorously. Cook for 2 minutes or until the sauce is smooth and glossy. Reduce the heat to low, add three-quarters of the grapes and simmer for 2 minutes. Adjust the seasoning. Remove the pan from the heat and stir in the cream. Serve the chicken garnished with the remaining grapes and the fresh herbs, and accompanied by the sauce. *Serves 4.*

NOTE Use 2 spring chickens or large poussins and shorten the cooking time by about 30 minutes.

Warm Monkfish & Persimmon

450g/1lb monkfish fillet, skinned and cleaned

3 cloves garlic, slivered

Few each dill and thyme sprigs

3 tablespoons olive oil

3 tablespoons sweet blackberry vinegar (see page 61), or blueberry vinegar

2 ripe persimmons or sharon fruit

Mixed salad greens and herb leaves

Few tarragon sprigs

Dressing

1 teaspoon whole grain mustard

4 tablespoons extra-virgin olive oil

3 tablespoons sweet blackberry vinegar (see page 61) or blueberry vinegar

1 teaspoon caster sugar

Pinch of salt and ½ teaspoon freshly ground black pepper

Rinse and dry the fish, make small incisions and insert the garlic. Arrange the fish in a dish and scatter the dill and thyme over. Blend the oil and vinegar, pour the mixture over the fish, cover and marinate for at least 1 hour, turning frequently.

Preheat the oven to 220°C/425°F/gas mark 7. Using a slotted spoon, remove the fish and place on a large sheet of foil. Strain the marinade and pour it over. Fold the foil over to make a

packet enclosing the fish. Put in a roasting tin, and bake for 15–20 minutes or until cooked. Meanwhile, slice the persimmons and arrange with the greens on a serving platter. Blend the mustard, oil and vinegar; add the sugar and seasoning. Remove the monkfish and cut it into diagonal slices. Arrange on the bed of greens and persimmon. Drizzle with a little dressing; serve the remainder separately. Garnish the monkfish with the tarragon. *Serves 4.*

Sole with Orange & Lettuce

450g/1lb sole fillets, skinned
3 tablespoons seasoned flour
3 tablespoons sunflower oil
3 tablespoons pine nuts
2 large oranges, peeled and segmented
3 tablespoons orange vinegar or oregano-flavoured wine vinegar
2 teaspoons orange blossom honey, warmed
1 large Cos or other crisp lettuce, shredded
½ tablespoon grated orange zest

Cut the sole into thin strips, about 7.5cm/3in long, and coat in the seasoned flour. Pour 1½ tablespoons of the oil into a frying pan and gently sauté half the sole over moderate heat for 1 minute; remove and drain. Repeat with the remaining oil and sole. Add the pine nuts to the oil remaining in the pan and cook for 1 minute or until golden. Add the sole, orange segments, vinegar and honey and heat gently, stirring, for 1 minute. Add the lettuce and heat for 30 seconds. Serve garnished with orange zest. *Serves 4.*

PRESERVES & SAUCES

Sweet & Sour Apricots

450g/1lb fresh firm apricots, halved and stoned
340g/12oz soft dark brown sugar
600ml/1 pint white wine vinegar
Few strips lemon zest
4 tablespoons lemon juice
2 sticks cinnamon, lightly bruised

Cover the apricots with boiling water, let sit for a few seconds, then skin and set aside.

Put the sugar in a wide shallow pan with the vinegar, lemon zest and juice and cinnamon. Dissolve over low heat, stirring occasionally. Add the apricots and simmer gently for 10 minutes or until the fruit is tender but still maintains its shape. Using a slotted spoon, lift the fruit from the syrup and pack into two sterilised 450g/1lb jars. Turn the heat to high and boil the remaining syrup until reduced by half. Pour the syrup over the apricots, seal and label. Leave to mature for at least 3 weeks. Use within 6 months. *Makes about 900g/2lb.*

Mixed Sweet & Hot Vegetable Pickle

1 each red and green peppers,
seeded and thickly sliced

4 medium carrots, cut in 2.5cm/1in
slices

1 medium cauliflower, in small
flowerets

3 pounds baby onions, peeled

1 whole head garlic, cloves peeled
but whole

280g/10oz salt

1 litre/2 pints malt vinegar

180ml/6floz water

200–250g/7–8oz sugar

1 teaspoon pickling spice

*I*n a glass bowl, alternate layers of vegetables and salt, finishing with a layer of salt. Cover and let stand until the next day. Drain, then rinse to remove the salt. Dry thoroughly.

In a stainless steel saucepan, bring the vinegar, water, sugar, and pickling spice just to the boil, stirring constantly.

Meanwhile, divide the vegetables among 6 warm, sterilised jars. Pour the hot vinegar mixture over the vegetables, making sure they are completely covered. Seal and let stand in a cool dark place for at least 2 weeks. Use within 2 months. *Makes about 2.7kg/6lb.*

Green Tomato & Coriander Relish

1.4kg/3lb green tomatoes, washed and chopped

1 large cucumber, chopped

2 tablespoons salt

3 cloves garlic, chopped

1 red pepper, seeded and chopped

750ml/1¼ pints white wine vinegar

115g/4oz soft brown sugar

1 tablespoon whole grain mustard

1 tablespoon coriander seeds

3 tablespoons chopped coriander

Put the tomatoes and cucumber in a bowl, sprinkle with salt, cover and leave overnight. Drain and rinse the vegetables thoroughly. Put them into a large pan with the garlic and red pepper. Blend the vinegar with the sugar, mustard and coriander seeds and add to the pan. Stir gently over low heat until the sugar has dissolved. Raise the heat to boiling, then simmer for 50 minutes or until the vegetables are soft. Stir in the chopped coriander. Cool slightly before packing into four warm, sterilised 450g/1lb jars. Seal and label. Leave to mature for about 1 month. Use within 6 months. *Makes about 1.8kg/4lb.*

Spiced Pears

900g/2lb firm pears, peeled, cored and quartered
Juice of 1 lemon
300ml/½ pint green peppercorn vinegar or cider vinegar
400g/14oz soft light brown sugar
Few strips lemon zest
12 cloves
2 cinnamon sticks, bruised

*P*ut the pears in a large saucepan with the lemon juice and
cover them with water. Bring to the boil over high heat,
then reduce to low and simmer for 15–20 minutes or until
cooked but still slightly firm. Drain the pears and reserve.

Combine the vinegar, sugar, lemon zest, cloves, cinnamon
and 300ml/½ pint water in the same saucepan, stirring over low
heat until the sugar has dissolved. Increase the heat to high and
boil for 10 minutes or until you have a light syrup. Reduce the
heat to low, add the pears and continue to cook for 10 minutes.
Remove the pears, strain the syrup and allow both to cool. Pack
the pears into two sterilised 450g/1lb preserving jars. Cover
with the strained syrup, seal and label. Use within 6 months.
Makes about 900g/2lb.

Rhubarb & Kumquat Chutney

1.1kg/2½lb rhubarb
Finely shredded zest and juice
   of 1 large orange
3 large onions, chopped
600ml/1 pint malt vinegar
300ml/½ pint orange vinegar
700g/1½lb soft light brown sugar

200g/7oz raisins
1 tablespoon mustard seeds
1 tablespoon mixed peppercorns
1 teaspoon whole allspice
340g/12oz kumquats, seeded and
   coarsely chopped

*T*rim the rhubarb into small lengths. Put the orange zest and the rhubarb into a deep shallow pan with the onions, vinegars, sugar and raisins. Simmer, stirring occasionally, until the sugar has dissolved. Tie the spices in a square of muslin and add to the pan. Continue simmering until thick. Discard the spices and pack the chutney into 8 warm, sterilised 450g/1lb jars. When cool, seal, label and leave to mature for 2 weeks. Use within 6 months.
Makes about 3.6kg/8lb.

Mango Chutney

115g/4oz raisins

115g/4oz fresh dates, stoned and
   chopped

1 red pepper, seeded and sliced

2–4 fresh green chillies, chopped

450ml/¾ pint cider vinegar

12 mangoes, peeled, stoned and
   sliced

450g/1lb soft light brown sugar

2 teaspoons crushed garlic

3 tablespoons peeled and grated
   fresh root ginger

1 onion, finely chopped

1 tablespoon salt

5 tablespoons lemon juice

*P*ut the raisins, dates, red pepper and chillies in a bowl. Pour in half the vinegar, cover and leave for 24 hours.

Pour into a wide shallow pan and add the remaining ingredients. Stir over low heat until the sugar has dissolved. Bring to the boil, then simmer for 1 hour or until thick. Cool slightly, then pack into three warm, sterilised 450g/1lb jars. When cold, seal and label. Use within 6 months. *Makes 1.4kg/3lb.*

FLAVOURED VINEGARS

Have fun combining different flavours. When sealing, either use a non-metallic lid or place a sheet of cling film over the top of a clean jar or bottle to separate the vinegar from the metal. Vinegar keeps indefinitely, but solids in the jar will discolour and eventually break down.

Nasturtium Vinegar

225g/8oz freshly picked nasturtium flowers

4 cloves

14 mixed peppercorns

1 teaspoon coriander seeds

1 teaspoon mustard seeds

2 cloves garlic, slivered

1 large onion, finely chopped

600ml/1 pint light malt vinegar, or white wine vinegar

Pick through the flowers to remove any dead or damaged material, then rinse lightly and leave to dry. Lightly bruise the spices to release their aroma. Divide the ingredients among four 360ml/12floz bottles or jars and cover with the vinegar. Seal and leave undisturbed for 2 months. *Makes 1.2 litres/2 pints.*

Rose Vinegar

1 part rose petals, preferably scented
4 parts wine vinegar

Rinse and dry the petals. Pack into small (300ml/½ pint) jars and fill with vinegar. Seal and leave in the sun for about 1 month, or as long as possible. Strain before using in salad dressings.

NOTE This is also ideal as a cordial. Stir about 2 tablespoons vinegar into 240ml/8floz water, sweetened with honey. For variety, make with wild violet blossoms and primroses.

Sweet Blackberry Vinegar

900g/2lb blackberries, picked over and rinsed
600ml/1 pint white wine vinegar
About 450g/1lb sugar

Put half of the blackberries in a large bowl. Add the vinegar and leave to stand for 24 hours. Drain the berries, reserving the liquid and blackberries separately. Pour the steeped vinegar over the remaining blackberries and steep as before. Return the first batch of berries to the vinegar, and leave for another 24 hours. Strain the vinegar through muslin into a large saucepan and discard the berries. Add 450g/1lb sugar for every 600ml/1 pint of vinegar. Boil over high heat for 30 minutes. Allow to cool, then bottle. Keep for 2 months before using. *Makes about 900ml/1¹/₂ pints.*

NOTE Adapted from *Summer Drinks and Winter Cordials,* Mrs. C. F. Leyel, 1925.

Rosemary Vinegar
450g/1lb rosemary sprigs, woody stalks discarded
600ml/1 pint cider vinegar

*R*inse and dry half the rosemary, bruising it lightly. Place the rosemary in a glass jar, add the vinegar and cover with a cloth. Leave for 2 days. Stir with a wooden spoon, then replace the cover. Leave for 7 more days. Strain the vinegar and discard the rosemary.

Using the strained vinegar repeat with the second bunch of rosemary, leaving it for at least 1 month. Pour through a fine sieve, bottle with fresh rosemary sprigs, seal and store in a cool dark place. *Makes 600ml/1 pint.*

NOTE This method also works for other herbs such as mint, dill, thyme and basil.

Blackcurrant Vinegar

450g/1lb blackcurrants
600ml/1 pint malt vinegar
About 700g/1½lb sugar

Discard stalks and any leaves from the black currants and rinse well. Drain thoroughly, then place in a large bowl. Mash the fruit lightly with a fork or the back of a wooden spoon, pour over the vinegar, cover with a clean cloth and let stand in a cool place for 3–4 days, stirring occasionally.

Strain the liquid through double thickness of muslin and measure into a wide shallow pan. For each 600ml/1 pint of liquid extracted, add 450g/1lb sugar. Place the pan over low heat and cook gently, stirring occasionally, until the sugar has dissolved. Bring to the boil and cook over high heat for 10 minutes. Cool, then strain into bottles and seal.

Keep in a cool place for up to 6 months. Once opened, use within 2–3 weeks. *Makes about 1 litre/1¾ pints.*

Index